LATE WORK

Rachel Blau DuPlessis

ISBN: 978-0-9997028-5-7

BSE Books are distributed by
  Small Press Distribution
  1341 Seventh Street
  Berkeley, CA 94710
  orders@spdbooks.org | www.spdbooks.org
  1-800-869-7553

BSE Books can also be purchased at
www.blacksquareeditions.org and www.hyperallergic.com

Contributions to BSE can be made to
  Off the Park Press, Inc.
  976 Kensington Ave.
  Plainfield, NJ 07060
  (Please make checks payable to Off the Park Press, Inc.)

To contact the Press please write:
  Black Square Editions
  1200 Broadway, Suite 3C
  New York, NY 10001

An independent subsidiary of Off the Park Press, Inc.
Member of CLMP.

Publisher: John Yau
Editors: Ronna Lebo and Boni Joi
Design & composition: Shanna Compton

Cover art: *Odd* (August, 2011) by Rachel Blau DuPlessis. By permission of the artist.

Contents

{crossed out in blue pencil on recto}
Time is {unreadable four lines}
But do, because we are not
Any other than
This   'peril
of the soul' & the impossible (?) completion
of Creation that times itself is
Form?

—Charles Olson in a letter to Robert Duncan

Late Work

1.

We meant what we said
       when we said we were
              running after language
as if we could never catch up.
       It was so fast,
          and the ground
              so distracting . . . so now what?
We're older.
       Can we now afford
          now to stop
running?
       Or must we make time even faster,
          faster?

What is the answer?
       Look under storms. Or even
          ask the dead. Since we are closer.

2.

     "Are you crazy?
Necromancy is forbidden"—
this to be said sternly, and panicked
given the temptations
of rolling dice,

casting sorts, reading cards,
drawing lots, scoping stars,
for who, faced
with the future,
would choose not
to try a little something?
Crystals at the ready.
Even the charms of a charm
chanted to the zodiac:

"Is late work enraged or is it pensive

is late work the same or is it different

is late work fulfilled, frustrated, fusty,

grateful, unreasonable, sickened or akimbo?

Late work has no time to spare,

breaks into torment.

No care for wounding—only making

late work cannot heal—rips asunder,

late work beyond, late work under

late work, fate work, fate work, late work."

3.

The dead, awaiting these visitors,
ready their workshop,
plane themselves down.

We touch their curly
          wood shavings
fondly, sniff that
          resiny smell.

Fuh! too much!

4.

Thus rebuffed, some of them sink,

          sulk plumb-like in small places

                    (stuffed sing-holes emit a whistling sound)

others find the liminal shunt, an odder hold

          on collapsed distance

                    and flush back and forth thru the pipeline

blowing intensely (like curtains in a beach house)

          chatty and self-centered as ever (amplification

                    is their middle name).

They want to tell you

       more than you can ever figure out

          or figure in.

"Do I know you?" "You seem familiar," they say

       while tangential wandering lights

          flicker and spin.

Plus regrets in patois

       sententious, particularistic, every third word

          unhearable, mumbled in different directions

(they're swiveling their heads right around).

       Often, they come back younger, which—

considering the condition they left in—is all to the good.

       Unless they died unanswerably young.

5.

Earth, air, wood, luminosity . . . .

So now I look to draw some water.

The faucet's loose

the screw's stripped

valve unfixable, pressure down to trickle.

This whole system needs a wrench.

Late work? I think we're on our own, now.

July 2016, July 2018

Shepherd's Calendar

1. January

How alarming our life is, how
it has invented ourselves almost out of existence
so the flicker
is hope that we, the humans, will survive
all this,
finding ways to act that can hardly be predicted,
much less faced. But can we—without the animals,
without the insects, without the fish, without the bees?
No, obviously not.
But we are arriving at that spot.

This endless Disappearance
(with that veil of time disappearing round the corner)
hides a question.
Is the thought only of trace?
Are things that apocalyptic?
Why is "the human" synonymous
with "hope"—given everything,
while at the same time,
most of this mess of place has been invented
and sustained by our selves.
Is it simply the technocrats whom we
must resocialize? remove? the demagogues?
At least could we offer a cryptic
outline of something—
sending unread letters out, documenting clouds of loss?

Poor planet I pray,
oh, slightly flattened ball of clay
(with its heavier iron core),
we its daughters (*korés*) and sons,
a *choros* of the powerless
and what to do?

In different languages, yet!
trying not to take a single way
into the multiplicity of Janus interests,
nested in vectors' multifaced splay.

2. February

This morning everything seemed silvery
for a time,
the leap-year day
featured a half-moon hung in the gray dawn sky.

But all our days
are *très riches heures*.
Pages of intricate borders and wee budding zones
frame this.

I make me, I make you
alert, I give you arcs of something back,
not complete but one-quarter satisfied
in its incompleteness.
Is that enough?

And every trace, a
paradox from A to
Zeno, makes another
longer-shorter spurt, a space in time,
as one approaches and never reaches
knowledge, but is filled with knowing
and the nobility of a stunned
quixotic effort.

And affect.
Also for A. It's
being a part of—. What?
That phrase has no single object; it's
everything. Being, B—
as part of OF.
One part will be called "air."
Part will be called "water."

And then within there is another shimmer, o.

3. March

Love, love!
          mini ode to the awkward heroes
of sexology,
stroking, fucking, tonguing,
          poking—while thoroughly
          amazed!

And to shepherds!
        try to be kind, not bitter.
Sit on the rock with your dog, the watcher
           and your proto-flutes whose notes
wobble among whiny microtones.
        Pipe foolish songs of glee
to grumpy, addled sheep
        (your selves).
Every character
      in the dream
         being part of you: Gestalt, Gestalt theory:
         Gesundheit!

And some characters resemble your friends.
      But why did you see him in a hood and cloak,
a cartoon glyph of death?
      Is it because
         another friend had died suddenly, simply
saying he "didn't feel well."
      But he'd "be OK in the morning."
         He wasn't.

         And since most materials
behave according to their defects and impediments,
      one question becomes
         how sheep receive these pretty songs
      of lambsy d'ivy,
amid real rocks and tocks and dust and rash-itch vines,
      the songs of places they never find,
         songs depicting their pastoral knees

deep in juicy true-green grasses,
while in reality, they hunch
in sneezy clumps, and pull the dumpy grass straight up,
and leave no roots at all.

4. April

O sylvan Why!
O woody How!
O bosky Whether!

O field of What!
Poetic Who!
O taciturn abyss.

'Tis e'en drecks swannery come round and round.
Grumbling sense lay dunkel, troubled; nixed sensual heft.
Who'd want to nix sensual heft?
Damn it! Start again!

Doats and groats, dots
cross stem streaked hatching
words scooped through thin streams and wispy days
of the looseness and seeking
root-worming, tendril rime
light and dark, broad brush and fine.
Come live with me, huh?
And whaddya think will happen next?

Five bridges, ten views, multiple weather allusions—
Mist, light rain, bright clouds, warm breeze,
longer nights and shorter, good and poorer fishing days,
poems scratched on silver-paper stars, and strung and hung
on trees.

In Ego
Arcadia.
Arcadia inside of me?
and you inside me, too.
Or was that Et in
Arcadia—ego.
Written on
that mossy marker—
tombstone for the grave.
Ergo?
Hence there is no revolution merely
via cleverness. Nor via piles of murder.
And everyone who's worth
their salt
will find this out.
Too late.

5. May

The fate of one's specificity
becomes the trace for another.

Crossing and recrossing
but traveling forward.

A ferry is comforting.
It appears as the "same journey."

Pulse and reverse.
Replay, double ply, reply, play
fast forward, the same, yet different.
A paradox of time—
the ferry seems just going back and forth
but always actually
keeps going forward.

I am ignorant of what you will see and hear.
But I wish you well, my future friends,
crossing on that sloshy ferry
just like once-me.

Let these words dissolve
into pools of unknowing
at what are, in fact, mutual
recognitions attenuated.

The ferry goes back.
You go forth
as once I did.
The physics of hope

involves witness and a toneless
sort of wordy-song, to mutter almost silently,
        perhaps a precarious strategy
yet it offers incitement to push on
to the next most useful and engaged
        between that you can imagine,

just as I tried to, evoking your going forth
as interleaved with mine—
to offer comradeship
        right across time.

6. June

Journeys precede restlessness and follow it.
Sounds start up suddenly and come to life in this telling.
                Bud comes just before city. Trace after dot.
Materials stagger forward.

Apparent nothings become rife with desire:
                icons, atoms, grunts of silence.
                        phonemes, testaments
rock back and forth and
                something comes forth
                from doing almost nothing

but teasing itself,
        humming beyond tunelessness.

A lot of nothing
a little something
a whiff of sexiness
    —and

Who is he? who is she? who xe and elseword on?
I love them all—
will love them better
when I get off—
for
it is
The City
I am
you are
and will be
sleeping With.
And In.
More yearning
more architecture
more configurations
and the smelly water
laps at the end of the street,
once you deplane or dock or land or
open the door, and see
what scintillation is,
and find the bridge

to now.

7. July

The melted dinosaurs made oil, they say,
they hunkered down, their past squeezed out
great slimy necks, a ten-ton stomp, a flying pump
swarming and eating. Very whiles. We.
Nothing. It was and many was,
they were.

Oil slick rainbow on the pavement,
a trace, to stain and steer
our funny monster lives
because we persistently "think"
we are the real-true center. It's clear
Copernican shock waves still reverberate.

So simple this subject and object plot,
like the "progressive" narrative
—the one where technology
is always an improvement—

do you really want
your fridge
dialing up your car
to tell you "you need milk"?
What if you're running down
on milk on purpose
to go on vacation, huh!

Did the fridge ever "think of that"?
The probable answer? unfortunately, yes.
Both options are now hardwired in
no matter where or how you choose.
Who can possibly get used to it?
I'll go—away—

but where?

Stamp. Stamp. We are tool-died;
we are turned out
and accessed for and
listened in on
(not listened to
but in on).

Yet still I remember
the pastoral, somewhat
quieter days
before internet, before
our own lives
spied
upon themselves.

Poor girl!
you do?

8. August

Crash of cluster chord.
Forearm goes smash on the keyboard
there is a 48-second
period of reverb
for that mess of stuff.

The sun hums
        with its million tones

coronal mass ejections, etc., and comets

swooshing down (that is, into our "down"), send

incredibly important "debris and fragment"

eventually named "us."

Different lumps of waves congeal:
extended, netlike, highly concentrated.
All things encode a frequency. The whole place
is resting energy and a fabulous (if unhearable)
cacophony.
This is the Shim of Space.
This is the Sound of Things.
Solidity
is what?
Flux—is what?
Everything proclaims raggedy stages
of being, everything spurts sound, and it's

all the same matter variously arranged,
and in continual movement—
pivoting here to now.

9. September

The window's sunny shape
makes a dark square
so that the hardness of this black light
marks you with an evanescent illumination,
"a fleeting but sharp pulsation
of historical awareness."
     Versus the endless humor of
"scientists were stunned to find
that the universe" is more
     irregular, more
          complicated, more
aesthetic, more
     redundant, more filled
with barely understood
     galactic languages
more articulate in its plurality of pulses
     and plethora of codes,
          its numerical mysteries
               of double primes,
     its ecologies of ode
          its elaborate amplifications
than—than what?

Well!
Than they had previously thought.
          Oh.

Or perhaps it's just a cliché
of journalism,
invoked to explain
what they still do not know
as if they really knew
something.
          Which they do
               (of course! who would deny it! not me!)
but only
      up to a point.

Poetry might be said
to know (or "know") the rest—
except that exact argument
is plenty self-serving.

But it's also pretty pleasing—like eating ripe figs
from your very own tree.

10. October

"The eclipse of the moon can be Googled"

is something impossible to have said in 1996

to the friends invited for dinner on the deck

who needed to know the time of the eclipse

because of their schedules the next day (busy)

plus the hopes that it wouldn't be cloudy, and so on . . .

There will be chicken paprikàs (in Carl Rakosi's recipe)

and maybe we will see

the blood moon
inscribed in the poem's
structure, in syntax that goes onward
interrupted
by solemn shifts
from the roll of the seasons, to moments
of intensity
that mark each other's wonder
but look forward unstintingly
to two temporalities
living and dead.

For the poem is only a dark door

opening straight out into nothing

which is another word for

everything.

11. November

I have stood in The Smallest Theater in the World.

Maybe it's not exactly what you think.

It is in Monte Castello di Vibio.

The Teatro della Concordia.

Its symbol is a pair of clasped hands, like friendship.

It was civic and optimistic when it first opened.

It was almost destroyed in the fascist era.

But it survived.

I'll bet you thought the smallest theater meant "me."

Well, that, too.

And now we can talk about the other smallest theater in the world:

You.

12. December

What will we tell the dead when we are dead
what will we tell the living when we are dead, and the living when living:

In fact—what will we tell any of them?

There's a blue-black zig on a yellow wing.
We will greet it
          in our own language
              while yearning to know its.

How many directions and times are there, and we enter
and inhabit however more.
I look forward, I look back.
I can't write this finally
because the whole
is about trace, a draft, a stroke, a kind of fear
a gap a hole in the fabric of the knowable
a lag a shred a tear.

A tolling sound—the trace
a clicking sound—of trace
the perfume of trace
the hair in the eye—trace
bloopy teenage letters—trace
lost dolls—trace
lost libraries—trace
the sense of evanescence, of time ticking in one's private body.
The trace of here am I, the trace of being there or anywhere.

Like memories, poems
          are often forgotten, or
      half-remembered, or

one knows the oddest bits
they flash and float, and the slits of barley
          or a little rising mist
          remind you of them, but they
are hardly there and can't be proved,
          and poems are written down now, or mostly,
or recorded and sung again
so this comparison is silly but it's
as if all your memories were
          one poem, the poem of the world
          adding other people's memories, gathering together
the placental mistletoe,
          the kiss abyss, so it's

all the world in a book—an ever-encompassing

poem-book to make and to hold

everything

and then the book goes

rogue.

2014–2016, July–August 2018

Incomplete Enlightenment

1.

The knife was raised
before there was an after.
He cried out, "Stop, stop!
"My name means laughter."

"But, darling boy,
no one said that laughter
comes only from joy.

"It could be
bitter, sardonic, dry,
a snort of knowing irony
before the drop,"

was the reply.

2.

The man in red
ripped pages from a heretical book.
This was the way
(some said)
intellectual life was meant
to be conducted,
standing firm in a baroque wind,

waging wars of absolute rightness
over a phoneme.
Burning the words
on every ripped-out page
until nothing was left
and that nothing
was also burned.

3.

If it were to be found,
                some scrap of that very paper

escaped, blown swirling
                in whirlwind heat
                                with the notation

                "man ripping book,"
it would be precious, yes,

only if people remain who
        know how to interpret it, or mourn it, or both,

                some readers

                        whose empathetic poise
                        and humane understan–

(here the scrap breaks off)

4.

Although perhaps
all *this* will show
is that someone had read *Tristram Shandy*.
And that someone else had understood
ashes.

But perhaps what it shows is
sometimes one must
actually
speak out.

5.

Sites were discovered accidentally
          by civic workmen,
                    digging a foundation by the side of a hill.

Strata were disturbed once they found
          a few ancient objects, and rooted around
                    for more, and then went quickly to sell them.

Soon after, contexts
          were no longer visible, levels were
                    unidentifiable, and

the lack of excavation records,
        the general absence of care
                made it impossible

to define or to refind the trace of this site,
        or the exact location
                where these artifacts emerged.

There might be
        other zones that this group had cultivated
                and where they had flourished.

There was a spring here,
        a crossroads there
                and hints of a parallel shrine.

These survive mainly
        as toponyms—local place names—
                in very odd dialects.

These uncanny phonemes are,
        until further excavation,
                the only record of this people's existence.

6.

Not accumulation, but a chain—
no, not even a chain,
but a random sequence of traces.

"Form is a process of forming
leaving a trace of its eventhood,"
a situation of self unselving.

Weird little pivots
that's your volta
talk to women.

7.

chucking, buzzing, lapping, chirping
all the charmed clichés of being
crossed with all the textured seeing

                    become marginalia

                    small hawk call

                    bugs streak by
                    not flying
                    but propelled by the sirocco.

Will you take all languages as sacred
(yes)
all texts as sacred
(naive)

                    How will you process
                    what you have taken?

8.

After the war
that was The War
there was a fierce postwar desire
(according to commentary from that time)
for a more "horizontal culture."

Now it's true we are living
after this war or that,
after exported wars, proxy wars,
quick wars, snotty wars, costly wars,

flyover wars,
brain-crunching wars,
ring-around-the-rosy wars,
the wars of all-fall-down
in mud and crazy blood.

But nothing of this now is actually
post war. One war is streaming
into another.

Quick-clock pulses
of agitated passage
are such
that a person suddenly

sees time, wasted
across the acreage (space)
where some part of any week—of any day!—is built
on devastation, year upon year.

What kind of culture do we desire
given that there is no letup
to war? No post war.
Do we know
what we are looking for?

9.

There were always fashions, this and that.
                    But enlightenment follows
                            a far different path—
            it's one that branches off.

Not courtly, not modish, a breath path,
                    a penetration of the dark, in dark.
                            Pushing stubbornly,

                            more than
                            partly
                            resigned.

10.

And one of those days
there were created atheists,
thank God, Blessed be His Name,
as should be said.

So I peck around the universe
one of the garden varieties of godless
Aufklarung chickens
tumbling over pebbles and grit.

        Chucking and clucking
        wonder ← despair
        wonder → despair

the things that began so pert and insouciant
then,
quick brushstrokes
and touches of light,
now
turn somewhat elegiac,
even *en plein air*.

        What can one little chicken do?
        We all gawk,
        squawk, fluff and crispen.
        Look out
        where.

11.

~~Hello, little ball of dust in the mirror!~~

~~Trace is not something else, it's you and here.~~

~~You know you are an item in an interlock of items~~

~~but like ecologies of your ignorance, you are~~

~~unseen on two planes: the sociopolitical, here,~~

~~and there from a space without a parallel consciousness, but one~~

~~that's not as intentional,~~

~~nor even malicious, when it destroys. This is one problem~~

~~of consciousness. Now.~~

2015–2016, July 2018

Quality Time

1.

I spent quality time after her memorial
reinventing banalities.

The absoluteness of her being,
here, then Photoshopped® out.

What is it that anyone
remembers? Most of the speakers

were not and could not be
eloquent. Everyone nibbled

at the borders of her life
and of the unspoken.

Nothing scandalous—just
you can't articulate it, any

of it, either in part
or as a whole.

Of course, memory itself
is one culprit: iterations,

inventions, recastings, thoughts
escaped, home movies, rifts,

pretensions, chains, scraps of fabric
and frozen evanescence.

Did you so believe in soul?
I didn't know! I thought the word was odd—.

Someone stripped away the black
of the beleaguered words,

to reveal the shadows
beneath their nakedness.

The heavy doors of travel
pivoted on hinges and turning points.

Sometimes hinges make a sound
like vermin. The mist

between landmarks encouraged earworms.
A Chopin étude, caught in a loop

and never resolved.
Or the "Chiquita banana" ditty,

pert, didactic, unforgettable,
a Potemkin village of kitchen pleasantries,

ethnic stereotypes and housewifery
under which tentacles

of collusion, massacre, preferential
access, policed economies,

and paramilitary activities
dug in, all far away from home.

You can see right away there are
      two stories—the palpable, but insignificant
            and the hidden, real enough but all obscured.
What? That number is patently
      ridiculous. Two says nothing. It's wrong already.
         It's certainly simultaneous, conflicting,
overloaded presences of "story," crossroads, the honey of personal life,
      one tiny part of a well-built honeycomb,
         done beautifully, with compassion,
            and the rocks onto which
some jump or fall—all that
      narrates nothing, all that loses everything,
      though a number like two or three might do to symbolize this
         so long as one doesn't forget intricacy and the networks
of privilege and collusion, themselves limiting us to the
      binary, the trifecta, the four cardinal points of mists
         often neatening or sweetening all of it, the lot.

Time's pale light upon the trees blinded the viewer
as the rushing stream rushed on.

Of course we spoke
awkwardly, a translation

without an original.
How could we have not?

2.

The poem, unwritten, is concealed by the poem, written.
It's kind of a disgrace.
There is a lot of blank paper in this notebook.
Perhaps it should be left there, empty.
Time is gone, emphatically lost.
Yet its feeling tone
persists.

That's what you say
because you want to say it—but
does it really?

Perhaps there is no choice.
This unwritten—reliably, as
a force that unwrites itself—
creates spray and backwash,
recriminations in the holes and crevices
that fill, some seasons,
with the powerfully dangerous tide
of what some person meant to do
and did
not.

Especially sediments of unfinished
stories, eroded stories—

Any solid page of print
is a bluff—or, I guess, that
is art.

It should truly be full of
ripped paper, holes,
elisions, burns, erasures,
white spaces
and actually

emptiness.

2014–2015

Everyday Life

Questions accumulate.

Answers not so much. I mean, believable ones.

But this whole work could have begun by describing a drift upward by the swallowtail butterfly. Should have? That would have been really nice. Maybe nicer.

"Then he and Claudius poisoned the tip of his fence."

I have real gaps in memory but am pretty good at provenance.

In 1967, I bought a copy of *Le Parti Pris des Choses* for the title. Meaning— that it's impossible to translate.

"MYnnn
MNNNNN
MI-YN
MINE!"
was her only comment after Day One of daycare.

The diaspora passed right down by the road in front of where I was standing.

He said he had been born, 1935, up the rocky hill before the war: "*Senza aqua, senza electricità, senza tutto niente.*" Absolutely no nothing.

On August 7, 2014, the day I read on *BBC News* of the conviction of two Khmer Rouge leaders for crimes against humanity, one day after the anniversary of the Hiroshima atomic bomb dropped on populations, and three days after one hundred years from the beginning of World War I, I made this sentence.

If the Large Glass was actually damaged by being shook up in a truck on the roadway over the Brooklyn Bridge, my icons line up with perfect synchronicity.

OK—so a throw of the die points to a number for a page of the dictionary, and the vocabulary is drawn from that precise page. But not exclusively. Did I get that right?

I find that vastly comic.

Do you know the "daddy longlegs" spider? Sometimes called "skull's head" because of its body shape. When it feels threatened, it does a shimmying stylized dance, like hula-hooping. Well, the point is, we have one in the bathtub.

Now they say Snakes used to have Little Legs.

Speaking up for things.

"Assume responsibility for your state of mind and all of your actions," said the Naropa University Right Action handout.

Tall order.

What are the "things" that "*choses*" encompasses? Is it people, too? words, too? days too? Probably so.

Homophonic *pretty party choses*. No, it's "*chooses*."

Some are committed to a category called "former life tales."

As if!

Taking the side of things.

Three blanks, beginning, middle, and end.

Two blanks, thesis and antithesis.

Read a good deal of *Skies*; woke to a big fog.

Then ask: what do I want. Because it's always doubled or more.

In my bad penmanship, "scene" and "scare" come out looking much the same.

New Jersey Turnpike, full-color, full-size billboard, classic photo of the Declaration of Independence with this statement: "I have a pen, I have a phone, I have some scissors. Paid for by David Pound."

David?

The Voice of Things? Bad choice.

The Stance Taken by Things. Attitude. Position. Even program. In the political sense.

Partisan of Things.

Why did we think it was up to us to take the side of things?

This may be all true, but it achieves the trappings of allegory.

If this reminds you of something, that's good. It doesn't have to be what I am saying.

I saw *Incomplete Enlightenment* twice. Once in New York and once in Venice.

That's probably accurate.

"This seems like not just an ambitious project, but one that's nearly overwrought."

Well, yes.

The random strewing of debris always moves me.

On behalf of things.

Now try to explain why "aqua melone" is not the translation of "water-melon" to a kid who knows the words "aqua" and "melone."

"Making Dying Illegal" is almost as brilliant a slogan as "RAID® Kills Bugs Dead." Less effective, though.

"If you don't like my attitude, don't read my T-shirt."

He spent six years honing the first six words of his dissertation. Then he gave up.

In the middle of my life, I found myself in a dark place with someone discussing "tax free munis."

"'Darkling' autocorrects to 'sparkle,'" said Chris McCreary.

"Poetry is the place where there is strangeness," said a well-known literary critic.

This text is made of traps.

An undoing as a doing.

Or was that the other way round.

Consequently, it is all strange, coming and going, no exceptions.

Things can speak for themselves. Really?

Further, with any disturbance in the atmosphere, the images shifted slightly.

Just *Things*. Even worse. What a minimalist fetish! Well, I used to have one, too.

Why claim to be speaking only of "things"? It is not true!

Still, don't pick up the bread knife when you meant to pick up the flyswatter. (Based on an actual case.)

"There are two models of literary history" is where I stop listening.

"I'll give you something to really cry about!" I always wondered what that would be.

"Two consciousnesses? That's all I get?" said Yolanda Wisher.

And, yes, "we are conscripts to our age."

The red gas pumps are called "Self."

The unthinkable events that have in fact occurred cannot be represented. Which creates an imperative to do so, and the way you do so is by a subtle sideways reminder.

But what happens if people have already totally forgotten the unthinkable and therefore cannot be reminded?

It *is* a strange and almost instantaneous modulation to go from having all the time in the world to having almost no time in the world.

"It is going to buzz during the reading because people are going to text me," said Ryan Eckes.

Ray Johnson is 100% my antitype. Except for the snakes.

"I will open your detachment later."

Every day takes up all my waking hours. Maybe 50% more.

Helen Frankenthaler said, "You tell it, and then it tells you." She was right.

"I simply have to nail my colours to myself and put up with the discomfort," said Roy Fisher. He was right.

"The nature of things" is a thick relationship—confusing and organized at once.

What is the form of my search? The overflowing of the poem.

Tap into the trunk of the world-tree. Boil down the bittersweetness. Then use the syrup as ink for a monoprint.

"A politicized sense of emotion," said Eric Keenaghan. That's what I wanted.

The only way to be turned is inside out.

Why was he indicted? Well, on his tax form, he had claimed all the citizens of Vietnam as his dependents.

We are incised and molded with the purling atoms of intergalactic deliveries and the suppurating politics of terrestrial unevenness.

Is a catalog enough? is a carton enough? is a tomb enough? is an archive enough?

The overflowering of the poem. This is the place where dark plum and black cherry jam tones intersect with crushed rock and gravely notes.

He dreams his work has been accepted by his dream publisher and wakes uncertain what to do next.

"You are at a crossroad." Just one? One road must cross another, no?

Yo! Don't talk back so much; quit your bargaining.

And that *was* a despoiling sleep.

Ash of the world's greatest age.

That would be us.

Philip Guston said, "They baffle me too. That's all I'm painting for."

Restless *poesis*, take your pungent fingers elsewhere.

No, I won't.

June–December 2015, June 2016; July 2018

Useful Knots and How to Tie Them

The medium

There is yearn, then there is yarn.
A strand is strung
from a number of yearns
twisted together.

Rope is twined
in a long building
by pulling cordage
out of sheer matter
in the endless twists of
how it matters, that it matters.
And what matters.
Space stands in for time.
Stringently.

The Overhand Knot

The overhand is
the simplest and smallest
of all knot forms
and the beginning
of many more difficult ones.

Instruction. Or Failure

This is one more lump
of the humped rope

inarticulate, snarled.
Stand ambiguates bight,
end-skeins twist.

Quick or careless tightening
results in a useless tangle.
If you do not follow the pattern,
you may get a different knot.
Even no knot at all.

Older Traction Points

Climbing
up fibrous ladders
and rope sways together,
you, and me, and others, specific,
needy, all unsortable,
there the ropy sway of acrobatic mountaineers
corded together, strung in a line,
toggled, cramponed.

And the climbing.
And the holding.
Bare ruinous coirs
threading athwart time.
There is everything, to begin.
But it seemed as if nothing can or will or could
(tense problem)
begin.

Comradeship

It is node of
tightened snags;
is a knot garden;
is a splay of *quipu*;
it is many-colored shimmers drawn
with embroidery silks
around padding for *trapunto*;
it is "a more or less complex, compact intersection
of interlaced cord, ribbon, rope or the like."
It is a power bundle
of peerless conjure and conjecture.
Impossible to do one metaphor only
given the sheer joy.
Of being like this.

But eventually one wakes
shaking out those silver streamers
from the nub, examining
their beauty, regarding them
suspiciously. Yet always
a little fondly.

Other moments
stayed vivid
in such flashes
as shoelaces.
Shoelaces!

As such!
What little tie will hold
when you are brought
to this edge?

The Fisherman's Knot

Strings follow knots,
knots demand strings,
and journeys capitulate
to restlessness.
Sounds start how-where
in birds, chk-warble,
or in the poetic silences
of not-real fish flickering,
but they exist for you only
when *you* hear them or see them—
a problem of consciousness in the world.

For if you began thinking
of real birds, real fish,
actual water enchained and linked to actual air,
that is, of really being here,
then your sense of implication,
of perhaps infinite otherness, would become
quite a bit more complicated.

Now seeing at least two
separate lines clearly,

should we tie them?
To tie, lay the two ends together
each pointing in the opposite direction.
Tie an overhand knot in the end of each
around the standing part of the other.

When drawn tight
the two knots slide together
and will not slip.
This will hold different strings
and extend them by
reciprocal pressures along the juncture.
The many times we want to use this
might surprise you.

The Cat's Paw

A forty-five-foot train runs like a river
from her Red Dress.
Foldings and loopings of material
matter
more than rufflings,
though there are ruchings
aplenty.
Then there is sheer
length to consider.

One is forced to reflect
on a Dress that Big.

Extent is flooded by its flag-bright color,
a singing carmine poured, pooling in sunlight.

If I were an engineer
I would schedule
site assessments,
public hearings,
maybe (though conceding
nothing) recalibrations.
But even without them, the ambition is clear.
A high wind roars in the valley of the seam.

The Cat's Paw is a hook hitch for heavy loads.
One grasps the two bights held well apart
twisting each away from you.
The strength occurs
in the double twist
and the oppositional direction
of their bearings.

The two loops thus pivoted into form
are brought together, tensile, vivid
and placed over one hook.

The walk on a blocked path

Itchy.
Itchy as the raw brown twine is
with the key strung around on my neck.

I walked along the obstructed path.
There was a drop on one side.
Twig piles and shagged-off branches
had been left thickly piled
to prevent more erosion.
But this
became a further impediment, a tangle
crisscrossed and cracking under foot.

Snakes hid in the side patches,
I, banging with a peeled stick
from the same woods
in which I was enmeshed.
I tripped. I pitched down.
I blamed myself.

Being

   a) in the middle
   of a woods, a
   wayward one,
   I, wayward,
   would design a way
   with words,
   but only stuttering
   way-off words.

   b) steadfast with the key still
   hung around my neck
   the twine-itch making a rash

as I walked the key
to the hidden mailbox
with its little keyhole
to see what was there.

Thus

The two struggled by design.
Neither could see the witless
witness, affirm the with-ness they denied,
though they were two ends
of the same rope,
wrestling with
themselves
locked into, snarled up and
roused beyond by power and by
seeking it. Or seeking
to be overcome
by contact and searing.

Cross and Twist

Is this possible—
being given, and driven by the knot?
this set of tracks
these woven intersections, intricate lines,
the turn and fold,
and the monumental desire and failure?

The ropes are scrolls
the scrolls are ropes,
Their rubric words remain bright red.
And these almost invisible bumps and swellings?
Nodules of commentary.

Any Regrets?

It was all necessary,
the desire, the loss, the itch, the anger,
the impossible push,
the separated cartilage.
And what now?
Acknowledge
that it was all necessary?
Or just refuse to concede?

String Theory

Inside there are three thick knots
by which one's past is tied:
carrick bend
(for heavy ropes
that cannot be tightened by hand)
sheet bend
(unties easily
without injuring rope fibers)
and sheepshank
(used to shorten rope).

So bright and clear
in this billowy air,
there is no sense of solidity,
no sense of crux or knot.
Yet it is all knot,
knots to which one is apprenticed,
knots pulling contradictions tight,
spun solids spiraling into void,
wads of matter,
the efficiency of the splice,
the memorable torque:

it was all there
although also all air.

Another Metaphor

In the closet
the basket falls over.
Nineteen spools of silky thread—
all the faded colors that chance had left here—
have rolled into a corner
noisily
on those old wooden spools
the way they knock about and ricochet
down the already tangled
warp of strangeness
pink notions, green cotton
mercerized,

thick black coat thread
a few pearly shirt buttons thrown in,
a hook, an eye, an allegory, a clew,
ball of old yarn rolled out
and traveling toward the center of the labyrinth.

Yards of yarn
loops of line,
texted and tangled
the wild loose threads, their unintended knots.
How did they manage such a colorful mix
from random thread spools knocking together in corners?
How could we not honor this urge for entanglement?

And intransigence—the thing that ties double knots.
Meaning that: First things are tied, then untied,
first raveled, then unraveled,
a joke
like flammable and inflammable.

So bound by the twine
that unwound in this labyrinth
quickened by the mystery of maze
we get tightened anew in the center of words,
clotted like blood and snared at the core
of former days.

June–October 2007; November 2015, July 2018

July 31, 2015

Every day has its story, a single minute would take years to describe, as would the smallest gesture, the careful peeling away of each word, each syllable, each sound, not to mention thoughts, which are things of great substance, thinking about what you think or thought or are thinking, and about what kind of thought it is exactly that thinks about another thought it's never ending.

— José Saramago

Woke to dream saying "have a nice day" and laughing.

The illusion of immediacy is a strangely duplicitous time/space in a poem.

The erotic shock is an ontological shock.

you? me? it?

Who was talking; who was laughing?

The word "a" and the word "day."

There is a white writing that is a black writing. It is ultimate writing. After that moment, there is no writing. When you come up to that wall, sometimes you must swerve back. In order to . . .

retain writing

as substance not fully crystallized

seize the DAY

let it trail

glisten of snail   silver path

crisping as it dries . . .

Every detail has its own multiple days
        within the days. The work asks

for itself—be listening to
                        obverse chronologies
                        specific provenance
                        the "niceness" of the day.

It thinks to mesh these little webs, their organic gears.

This will prove beyond us.

•

Well, there's speaking, there's silence, and then there's middle ground.

He said "Whereof one cannot speak, thereof one must be silent."
    Elegant.

In some moods, yes, of course that's true,

        and modest, too, which is why

        it is elegant.

        But not always so true, not so completely.

An implication   hovers resonant   and yet unsounded.
    How to indicate your wonder without words.
How to speak, silently:
    how to approach this through another subject . . .?

"Whereof"/ "thereof" leaves some space or . . . offers hints . . .
    How?
    Retune the topic by another vibration.
    Another: phatic mmmm's   upward or downward
        That's one sound, not strictly speech.

        If being totally unsounded is desired there are

        looks, glances, twists of body charm,
        an annoyance only apparently suppressed
                or a smile; smiles come in various tones.

I was holding, keeping precious, sheltering these
acts of not-speaking, signs telling something without voicing.

They were made of feelings-as-gestures not marks-on-paper
or claims-out-loud.

All were silent.

Yes, I am "misinterpreting." Being "too literal."

                Still it's good to be reminded
                of signing without talking, of the limits of speech.

Of the "hard problem": not blabbing about what we actually do not
    know.
Though without indicating and talking, how do we know that we do not
    know it?

So finally,
this famous statement, at the end of his now-famous book, rests
on the argument-sealing authority   of decisive, proud, patriarchal
    humility.

●

Color blue, of articulated bright glass in a rinsing changeable sunlight.

"Blue" he said "is a stimulating negation"

bringing the question back to Nothingness

                as fast as any thoughts of Being also does.

Whereof one does not acknowledge all of the above
still
while sitting amid long grasses,

I imagined the plants drawing their own marks

by the play of sun-shadow. By their movement in wind.

A form of silence with little visual swishes

quite

informative.

Changes (of meaning?) in the turns of light.

All the above demands
nothing but one's attentive
(if provisional) (also temporary)
presence.
So wake up.

●

Aphorisms, paradoxes and
fragments

will be situationally selected,
then strung together as if a continuous text

to document something
of what we are seeing
(even with blind spots)

        rubbing up against
        hearing (with silences, too
        from deaf patches)

all exfoliating depths and breadths of the detail,

the array
genial—disjointed linking of a flux of words
fusing   sometimes refusing

never one single event but markers and traces
joined to . . . the clustered imprint . . .

of a constellated multidimensional other,

provoking a poem with its memories of effaced histories,
of the half-remembered, of another trace . . .

etc.

●

But then this became pity, pity, and rage
that earth treats us like its fertilizer

and we / us continuously debating that point
in RE: treating ourselves thus

        with the desire for memorials and memories of special deaths
and yet endless and unmemorialized
                        "expendables"
                        murdered by their kind.

Earth

"should not
            cover this blood."

"O earth, do not conceal this blood. Let it cry out . . ."

simply like that

        those piles of matter set within the piles of time.

But earth will generally not concede the point.

        For if uncovered we'd all be totally awash in blood
and speaking nothing but blood.

●

                        Look at this or that
ferocity foisted on the skeleton of our time, but
which ferocity should we choose?
we want to rip some bones of bones apart
and hit and smash where others stand
but want somehow to have our flesh unhurt.

Look how we embody contradictions!

You have the right to remain silent
as accused
of irrevocable
apathy   stupidity   generalize as you will.

•

Then the dark comes to wrap the day and to cocoon
          the body round, a body ready
                    to be consumed by yet another dream.

The insomniac holds tight,
          trying to sleep straight through a single night.
                    Can't win for losing.

Return (from whence?)
          terrified and sleep barely had (achieved, registered)
                    amid the intense
                              clamors of dawn

here, where there is no place
precisely nominated "place"
only the dot of universe
out-spun in diffusion.
But I live in that space.

Now what?

•

The desire to create total alterity
(I already have the critique of that, OK?),

and I mean total, like nothing ever before
in language or vision

which also speaks or signs
(I'm on it, OK?)
directly into heartsick minds
and discourses stuffed with
suffering;

this desire is trying to transmit to me
a transformed alphabet, an altered language,
a structure beyond anything ever seen before.

Such desires, such energy-roars—
whole galaxies, dark matter
and other life forms pulsing
over and inside of one tiny person
inside a tiny day—

leave a smallish souvenir here,
I call it "a poem."
It lives within the world as such,
the world of wasted wretched blood.

Poem: as probably
another remnant
of the "weird life
enabled by
astrobiology"

●

It's like the "ideal

day" (or so I used to think—

now think again)

entirely blazing.

entirely aflame

so entirely composed of light

that no one would ever see

the shadowy nothing "I"

with all its magpie doubts and darks,

in any of the shifting deictic bits

in which it does, in fact, exist,

the distracted, uncanny but familiar "I"

pointing continuously and pivoting

here and there

now and then

today and yesterday

even to the 31st, the 1st and

various piles of numbers—it's

all the It, actually,

when you come right

down to it.

●

Yet however simple (it
        is one single day),

it's still able
        to work itself

and its baffled occupant
        into ecstasy.

> *supposedly July 31, 2015, as an assignment—but not quite*

Per Se

1.

Pause. Let this stanza

remain almost blank.

> a silent place
> for the reverb
> of unheard

~~Spaces.~~   ~~Words.~~

2.

A thousand-odd pages were already articulated

as if a "prolegomena to itself."

Now what?

3.

Ask the letter A,
and it may tell you
to continue.

Sortie—ledge.

Stand

right on that bluff,

that edge.

4.

A

struggles from itself
from whiteness into
black with-

ness, or witness or

an opposite, a precipitate

rush to deny. But then comes

Z

its end zone. Something

unsafe, turning itself endlessly into zero—

a void
but filled with searches—

as if
sexy ache and
contraction pulses
and rasping end-time breath
         were held incipient.

        Fullness fills
            these times,
                then empties.

5.

"A" is the liquid sibyl
        generating melodious
                diphthong swings.

Whenever she swivels forth,
        her sexy tune begins on
                Aaaaay and ends on Yuhhhhh.
If just one letter swaying
        rhapsodizes everything, A to Y,
                then, as with π,

there's unresolvable
        resonant extent.
                The universe

is built upon a shim.
    It's made of language
        stacked upon languages

codes upon holes,

    microtonal twanging range,

        orphic and eurydic communiqués.

6.

School kids chanting "A, B, C" used to say
"ampersand the end."

A singsong "X, Y, Z and
&," as such,

as if that extra pinch of leaven
achieved a quasi-letter 27.

Per se points to an "and"
that stands for just itself

and everything else.
That's when the mouthful

"and-per-se-and"
becomes "ampersand" and

declares an endless series
endlessly open.

Things
can go on and on.

In this spirit
I'm trying to respond.

Should I say: "as much
as I can"?

7.

A similar situation

infuses thirdness;

kids swaying

"one—two—**THREE.**"

Emphatically.

Take *Tre* as sign to seek the trace

beyond any word's declarative enigma,

into the root space:

The drifting round of the mark.

8.

There is nothing either big or small,
the scales have shifted, both are simultaneous.
There are traces, there are days, and
both include the each.

And if you say *yes*
        you generate an opposite
                that might be *no* or might be

not-yes, a-yes (neutralized),
        un-yes, re: yes,
                ethical-no

or *both/and*
        and all the same-same
                round another way round.

9.

"I should be more bold, for anyone who is not with me

here

will long ago have ceased to read the book."

10.

One conjuncture of dust in an era of shame.

One single alphabet turns and twists

among the rest.

And if that, then what?

What did I come to show you

more than this?

11.

Syllogism, mid-January day glow.

Earth is trying to shift its light;

it's making a special effort, right this minute. Now.

"Hey poems, we are free to go."

January–August 2015, July–August 2018

Mackle, Shard, and Trace

1.

So what's the point?
      To outline the trace of wandering,
the stain of one small life
      among the elements

spent (*inter alia*)
      counting green, blue, orange marks,
      the painted infrastructure signage
      on sidewalk or asphalt
or seeing a twig
      frozen half in half out
      of an ice-crusted puddle,
or charting instances of smudge
      and crease
      and lines counter-crossed against
      the page-white stucco—
            in a blare of sunlight.
Too bright to be read.

Or like that spot
the double blur of type

that fold-over on the page
swallowing up some words
      slicing the others

so that when you unfold
the misprinted paper
a wedge of whiteness
empties deep inside the book.

2.

Found the shards mackled with mold
black on the unglazed tile,

found trees dappled with lichen.
Silvery symbiosis,
one part fungus one part algae,

and now the third term
just discovered:
the yeast conjoining these conjunctures.

3.

And if the mouse or vole or dog
could speak trans-
planted squeak or sqwuff, would we
believe—could we listen?
of what their languages are? in whose
translation? what did they say to us?
who has ears to hear it?

O, I am an owl in the wilderness
a little owl in the waste places
a lonely bird on the tower top.

4.

Traces make a triple
overwritten language.

Any palimpsest
protests all singleness.

Understanding comes slowly,
a reading beyond, in trepidation,

while hearts of extinct animals
beat with cancellation.

5.

The trace
may accept its own inevitable erasure
as flimsy discredited smudge,
as stranded wisp of other times.
But does not accept the erasure of enormity.
Though it doesn't generally get to choose.

6.

The trace is never without meanings.
It's us who may not know the meanings.
If things do speak among themselves,
we may never know, or never acknowledge it.

7.

Yet "trace" may avoid the question
          of why,
may celebrate the
          one thing left
the diary recovered from the rubble
          the hidden painting rediscovered
but never talk of who and how.
          We get so grateful for the smudge that's here
that we don't acknowledge the fullness
          that was.
Rupture. Destruction.
          Should one really be so grateful?

8.

Even the LETTER is mackle,
a black glyph set so that a wall opened.
(A book is a portable fresco.)

And each letter's tangle
            declared itself at the middle
    of one dark word
                after another; the black iridescent sheen
                activating multiple angles.

9.

Poetry is not the poetic.

Poetry
        is something smaller, with
        "an unlikely smattering of themes."

A kind of Singing Smudge.
        Erasures, excavating slightest blurry trace.
        Recoveries within Effacement,

Mackled bits of Being
smatter smatter smatter.

July 2015—July 2016

Angelus Novus

1.

It's A Strange Angel!

A NEW & **improved** angel!

Chicken-footed claws and finger feathers,
a perfect poultry type.
Raglan sleeve-y wings
with a sigh-nage, hmmmm.
Him. Her. It. They.
Ange or angel-us.
An angular build,
spikes poke half-wise as its puzzle parts—
triangles, churches, knife blades
and/or mountains.

Tri-ages. A wire-line's the shadow
of its doubled halftone self.
It stands in clarity. It stands in blur.
Its face is a scroll, or maybe a lion
with intelligent snout.
You'd think, given strength and virtue,
things might just work out.

But its animal eyes fly to the side,
crooked right,
left askew

slid to where
the remnants brew.

This is your body on fear.
This is your body on dread.
Eyes pop out of its head.
Eyelids widen and pupils dilate
hair rises, muscles vibrate.

Though it shudders, it is fixed.
It's staring
at the wrong ends
of pick-up sticks.

2.

There is a painting by Klee called Angelus Novus. *It shows an angel who seems about to move away from something he stares at. His eyes are wide, his mouth is open, his wings are spread. This is how the angel of history must look. His face is turned toward the past. Where a chain of events appears before us, he sees one single catastrophe, which keeps piling wreckage upon wreckage and hurls it at his feet. The angel would like to stay, awaken the dead, and make whole what has been smashed. But a storm is blowing from Paradise and has got caught in his wings; it is so strong that the angel can no longer close them. This storm drives him irresistibly into the future to which his back is turned, while the pile of debris before him grows toward the sky. What we call progress is this storm.*

—Walter Benjamin

3.

To ask which way
the wind is blowing
is not a 60s joke.

This says it's from a "Paradise"
generating wreckage, but
suctioning backward to the future.

To ask in what way
its wings will ever close
is not another joke.

The wreckage lies
in the same quarter
(in front of it) as Paradise.

What dreck is coming from the blast?
Will the future be the same
as this wrecked past?

4. Some questions, some answers

What does have the power? A storm.
A Power Surge. From whence? From

Paradise! And where is Paradise? Yes—ask!
is it coming in the future, or lurking in the past?

Is "Paradise" the goal before us
or the theological back?

The messianic Will says "Paradise" (glimmer)
is coming forth, full monty futurial.

While Paradise was (cue glittery shimmer)
once angels' home, this Paradise

is modern and gives rise to storms.
It's not a place of peace, but turbulence.

How can this be? Is every image wrong?
Is Paradise Malign? Is Angel Powerless?

Are these names obsolete, fiat, functionless?
We seize up, freeze up: thesis, antithesis,
paralysis.

5. Almost the same

Why does this angel have fewer powers than us?
We perceive a "chain of events." It perceives "debris."

We project a narrative linkage.
It perceives "catastrophe."

Why is the wreckage apparently invisible?
I mean: not rendered in this scene.

Did everything shift in the twisting swirl
of a funhouse twirl called "history"?

In the realm of angels, is there no logic, no cause
and effect, nothing syllogistic? Is the answer "yes, not"?

How to imagine the motives of any angels;
then how do these get thwarted? And by what?

The angel would like to stay, its mission
to institute justice by heavenly fission.

Nonetheless, it is doomed to hover
paralyzed inside this ever-darkening loss:

which is—Whatever Comes when winds
from so-called Paradise double their Force.

6.

This thing is not a picture exactly,
It is one monoprint, unrepeatable.
Mainly not to illustrate
but to parallel us and travel together.
These glyphs are flat as forms of fate.

Ledgers
unreadable records

accounts of daze
barely having time to leave
their ugly detritus
before more arrives.

The stakes that high.
Were always so.

Almost unrepresentable is everything.
That's why you might say

that Benjamin's glyph—taken from Klee—
is "illogical." If you can't represent this,

you just can't. But there's the joke.
It is what it is, like IAM/IAM

stuck in the throat.
So what's to say in face of all this?

Let them eat cake.
Let them choke.

7.

Consider cinders, consider the badger
bludgeoned.

Irreducible, implacable,
inadequate, insightful,

not enough, never enough
but enough after all,

enough to be unbearable.
Already "ruins." The line

tightens. Can the "right"
words get gasped out?

Get grasped? Shards
on the shard pile testify.

8.

My vocabulary didn't do anything
in the way of killing me.

It was the findings.

I have seen an incandescent lightbulb that had angel wings wired on it—
and it was "Style"—pretty pricey—a designer fixture. Cute. A plain old
lightbulb, and some white feathers. Almost a cartoon. But it was true.

Do angels have money? Hold it; that wasn't the question. But I couldn't
read my scribble. This was it: "Do angels have memory?" Just a note,

straight out of Dante. The desire for brightness and luminosity, compared with our diurnality. They don't go into our darkness? Except when given a mission. And then they never stay.

But who really cares about "angels" except you've just spent a few hours in yet another museum. Although it is nice to see them wander around the world in the imagination of various cultures—those pretty and elegant androgynes whose feathery wings are sometimes covered with eyes. If they had that many eyes—and all those rainbow stripes, they probably don't need either memory or money.

They simply give the message they have been given. Someone tweeted: Don't bomb Syria; glitter-bomb Russia. Do you remember this? It was a specific moment.

Plus I just learned about mica. It's mined almost exclusively by children twelve and under. In India. And often mined illegally. Where does this leave us? Or actually, in our part of this, our collective world: where does it leave anyone?

9.

We live amid documents
a new batch every day, vital
to document something

of what we are seeing.
Hence a poetry not solely

"poetry"—do I have to spell
this out?

We are on energy alert,
but on a short fuse for qwik illumination
so then the poles
swerve to depression with disgust,
swerve back, practically electrocuted with despair
and reanimated, jolts of force, more power
plus unsought powerlessness.

Our angel was once rooted in its clarity of purpose
and grew in light
but that brand of angel declined,
was withdrawn from the market,
ripped from its root,
wrenched out
of shifting soil and in straining winds.
Thus the angel found itself
deep flung across the place once home.
Splayed, and played
out.
It got worn, raggedy and frightened,
and so it looked
like us.
The Angel-Us.
Yes,
spell
it
out.

10.

A project is a desire, altering
itself as it goes, shadowing
the names it thought it had, tracing
the words behind the words
which are the only ways to know.

To live among quotations makes
everything exegesis, which ennobles solemnity and
convergence.
One pitches down the incline of the scroll.
Interpretation is a mode of clarity,
and maybe (very loosely)
reverence.
Destiny.

11.

We live in nomadic
unfulfillment.

Therefore I am the philologist of the trace
and I am not I
hello, goodbye.
To read trace is violation;
not to read disvalidates whatever the mark might give.

We stare at the plethora of texts.
The trace is a smudge of flattened historical time.
A sullying—hedged spaces
the hard-to-clean grease of endlessly
bad politics. Ecologies fucked.
Or "challenged" to breaking.

Persons like numbers but
unnumbered,
picking at shards
thrown off by cataclysm
lying among those broken parts
and speaking in the voices of the dead
so? so? so? Speak?
Nothing. Again nothing?
What is beyond that sublime?

Something. For which there is no
genre, but swiveling pressures on words
from words
blowing and blasted at every turn
like mini-angels.

The time of now is palpable; it is the source.
Tense and restless, twisted lot and cowed,
is it possible to vow?
To gather up our nothingness as force,
to enter the dark tunnel of our time once more.

2013–2016, July 2018

Summer Poem

Fuchsia thistle, purple artichoke,
      lavender-blue lavender
            and the bees—yellow pillow-

pollen on their thighs—
      osmotic hammerlock
            of thorns and sweetness:

someone can get lost
      in this plethora of signs.
            Welter, welter, obvious pleasure, and
               endlessly the hum of song.

Yet bees are sick of men.
Bees are sick of humankind.

So failed justice and political deaths
      are what we have,
            that so-called human

mark.
      Failed justice
            and murderous deaths.

            Countable.

            Unaccounted
            Uncontainable

•

Shiva is the seven days of formal mourning
                    the moon breaks into the river like crusts
shiv, slice
shiv—knife
sitting with the slice is shiva.

              The blur from poetry sopped into elegy.
              Can't we account for the whole Real?
                    Harder than you think.

              For once inside "poetic utterance"
                          it's often creepy.

"They tell us what to feel, and what to say.
These feelings are rewarded with grants."

That's a paraphrase
of what Lorenzo told me.

        But
                    to talk of the unspeakable or render the blight?
                    To get the detail there and the conflicting one
                    both right—not even "formal"?
                          to express rage, gather powerlessness,
                                pivot it, and then try to strike?
                                to acknowledge hope and the failure of hope?

Isn't this experience ours? isn't this

what we know?
all rough and problematic?

How to make the stuff we live right now— into "art."
Or, how to stop thinking about art.

●

The rifts
      are reclaiming the ore.
      as if earth were taking back its own
      forget smelting, forget processing
            forget artifacts, forget the intricate claims of human craft.

The rifts are taking the ore back to the mine.
Even before the mine, back to the Crevasse.

Such rent and scar
such cavernous abyss
700 drowned
      140 exploded
         40 shot.
              One cold-cock murder
                and then another.
                    And it continues—towers of
                    human sacrifice, one over one.
                    built of water, fire and the gun.

•

How inside a flower before it opens
          is flower air.

How inside us is the ayre
          of despairingly hopeful trek.
                    But breathless from climbing.

How "birds
are essentially feather-fringed bubbles"
                    buoyant from interior capsules of air—

Maybe we are
still en route to the something better
and not so exacerbated
and stuck. We have our inner air. But we have to breathe it.
We have to choose and calm and analyze the routes.

What is the form for an intermittence of imperfect
understanding? mingled with despair and rage and
tired fear.

More than "ungainliness"—though, yes, that.

OK—the fragment—but is there something else?
          Moving fragment into syntax
moving syntax into fragment
          moving smudge into song
                    moving trace into day—.

Lists, lists—now to break the lasts!
Could there be more modes,
         could there be other
         routes to broken
         stalwart thoughts?

●

Auric subtlety
pulses beneath the square hardness of light.

              "It does not matter whether you are ready,"
                   it's happening.

              If you take landscapes
              to "talk"
         about states of mind (we have seen this before)

                   take dreams—the twisting downward
                   spiral (evocative enough,
                        we know about this move)

But what is discovery?
                   A plastic bag puffs high
                   in bright blue sky
                   ahoy—this is bad.

This world of products that "we've" built
         via the poverty of others
         via plastic living

dragging sodden thru the ocean

The fish will not (we hope)
the whales? will they?

We are answerless.
We count on the intelligence
of creatures we have long
discredited.
Disinherited.
We need them now.

●

Hearing these voices
        come through mind
                        without resolution   without clarification without

syntactic packing,   half off   grief-stricken   inchoate piles of
        unresolved rage

Our rhetoric is as bereft as our thought.

Where is discovery?

How should we sound?   Not the way we did before.

●

"**Our** poetry has feeling,"
said the well-wrought man.
He was standing
in the "Center,"
on a greeny hill
inside a repeat.

My poetry—what is it?
I placed a smash of wordlings
and of dust. Unsmoothed.
Unmoralized.

Still, mine was also filled with feeling.
Overflow. But mine was not
as round or nice
upon that hill.

●

How many
        painters have
            decided to destroy their work

one day, in the day, that day
            they finally do it. They rip the paintings
                shred the canvases and claim
                to have no image left, in order

        to erase all memory of that phase of work.

There has to be making beyond the market,
      they say. Or I am starting now from zero. Or
           I reject my former direction; I didn't like
I'd gone down
      that path
           and couldn't stop without destruction.

That personal vendetta
denying your saturation,
           in what you did or made before.
                It's an exciting gesture—that's for sure.
                X-treme Art.

The question to me
      —is how to go on from this, not to trash it.
           But really—the other question: is this my cowardice?

•

"It ain't over"

           shocked from my chair as the fighter bombers fly out

the air is trembling, yes, we are on the flight path

of a serious airbase in a serious time filled with serious lies.

           We are all choked on human sadness

"no, it AIN'T over
till your brother counts the votes."

But I don't have that brother.
I have another kind of brother.
"It ain't over till we find that brother."

We are together, uneven and unevenly;
we are that dust. We are those motes.

●

Raising

the question of dervishing inside an already implacable dizziness

with human ratio

kill ratio, or the costs, or the calculus

     another kind of thinking

          far off the limits of the poem's qualified language.

so today
     that was that.

●

and mourning halfness and quarterness and minims.

But who cares about your little life except
you, a family few, a friend or two
given
the politics of "our time"
the politics of space and resources   sexual politics   race-laden
politics
the politics of agency   the politics of no agency   protective
politics
proactive politics   water, water, water

daily politics, weird shit,

encrypted politics, complicity and loss—

International endnotes
questions of ethics—
the ink blue idea still wet and luminous

abruptly drying into thin crust on the page.

The haiku (allusive) in which it's all buried
the faded memory of shining forth.

●

Gaily marched around the White House and its park
this, once upon a time.
ringing the rows of riot police

trails of images
        could we have stopped the bombing

slowed it perhaps, perhaps we even did
eventually some change for a while—

      humans are profligate with themselves
           as if they didn't matter

some little person
      just blown away
          like anyone—with some unbelievably legal

or carefully nurtured thing. A loaded gun. A chemical spray.

•

           I am another explosive-feeling dot

hunkered down some where
        how do I live
      do I hope in despair?

or despair with spurts of anger?
      what do I say now? is it this?

Snarled like a knot in bidirectional corruption
      tightened within this are words and ways to proceed
      that cannot yet emerge.
          I certainly cannot simply say "o sing."

Yet this poetry has feeling,
along with every other possible thing.
This is one way to begin.

•

The Dead.

Of Winter.

People say this when it's very cold and grim.

But this

is the dead of summer.

That's not what we generally say.

 It's just what's really happening. Now what?

Let more in.

July–August 2016, July 2018

Notes to the Poems

The epigraph to this manuscript comes from a 1960 letter of Charles Olson to Robert Duncan as edited by Robert J. Bertholf and Dale M. Spender. I take it as a trace that can barely be tracked and is yet palpable, as a reminder of concerns, like time, central to this manuscript, and as an homage to our elders and to the process of transmission in which we are all engaged. *An Open Map: The correspondence of Robert Duncan and Charles Olson*. Albuquerque: University of New Mexico Press, 2017, 166.

Shepherd's Calendar

Section 9: "a fleeting but sharp pulsation of historical awareness." Todd Carmody, "The Banality of the Document: Charles Reznikoff's 'Holocaust' and Ineloquent Empathy." *jml* [*Journal of Modern Literature*] 32, 1 (Fall 2008): 86–110. Citation on 90.

Incomplete Enlightenment

Incomplete Enlightenment is the title of a miniature of a man standing (and perhaps meditating), by the contemporary Pakistani artist Imram Qureshi.

"Form is a process of forming leaving a trace of its eventhood,"
Derek Attridge, apparently in chapter 1 of *Moving Words: Forms of English Poetry*. Oxford: Oxford University Press, 2013, but I was not able to refind it.

Everyday Life

About the throw of the die: Peter Quartermain, in *Stubborn Poetries: Poetic Facticity and the Avant-Garde* [Tuscaloosa: University of Alabama Press, 2013], describing Louis Zukofsky's procedures for *Thanks to the Dictionary*.

Skies is a work in *The Alphabet* by Ron Silliman.

The billboard—couldn't make that up. Seen November 2014.

Incomplete Enlightenment, as above, is by the contemporary Pakistani miniature painter, Imram Qureshi.

"Conscripts to our age" is cited from W. H. Auden's *New Year Letter* (1944), line 331.

Helen Frankenthaler, speech at Harvard/Radcliffe in 1976. Cited in *Giving Up One's Mark: Helen Frankenthaler in the 1960s and 1970s*, curated by Douglas Dreishpoon. Buffalo: Albright-Knox Art Gallery, 2014, 7.

Roy Fisher in *Jacket* [1], # 35.

The tax resister during the Vietnam War was the poet Henry Braun.

Citations from poets, McCreary, Wisher, Eckes, Keenaghan, all former students.

Translations of the title by Francis Ponge, passim. Some have been used by various translators, the others are mine.

"They baffle me too." Philip Guston, from a letter he wrote to Ross Feld, self-cited in his "Talk at 'Art/Not Art?' Conference," from 1978. In *Philip Guston: Collected Writings, Lectures, and Conversations*. ed. Clark Coolidge. Berkeley: University of California Press, 2011, 280. Curiously "That's all I'm painting for" from the citation in my poem is not in any of these sources. There's clearly another source.

"Bafflement" as Guston's motivation is stated in a number of other essays in this collection. These include pp.110 (from 1969) and 153 (a talk at Yale Summer University School of Music and Art, 1972).

Useful Knots and How to Tie Them
The found language in this poem, including its title, is from the pamphlet *Useful Knots and How to Tie Them,* a handout from the Plymouth Cordage Company in Plymouth, Massachusetts, copyright 1946, and distributed by Louis E. Helm Marine Company in Wethersfield, Connecticut in the 1950s.

"A more or less complex, compact intersection of interlaced cord, ribbon, robe or the like." is the dictionary definition of knot from *The American Heritage Dictionary.*

The Red Dress that makes an appearance in one section is by the artist Beverly Semmes, 1992, seen in the Hirshhorn Museum and Sculpture Garden, Washington, DC.

July 31, 2015
Epigraph—José Saramago, *Raised from the Ground* (1980). Trans. Margaret Jill Costa. NY: Houghton Mifflin, 2012, 53.

Person saying "Whereof"—Wittgenstein, the final proposition of *Tractatus Logico-Philosophicus.*

Person on "blue"—Goethe on color.

Invocation to "earth"—Job 16:18.

Per Se

Title and Section 6: Discussion of Per Se by Anu Garg, *A Word a Day* website. "Today's term makes an appearance in the word ampersand which is a corruption of 'and per se and.' What does it mean? Earlier the '&'symbol was considered the 27th letter of the alphabet. Yes, they used to say 'A to ampersand' instead of 'A to Z.' It'd be awkward to recite the alphabet as ' . . . X Y Z &' (and what?), so schoolchildren reciting the alphabet would end it with '& per se and,' meaning the symbol &, by itself, is the word 'and.'"

Section 3: Colleen Lamos on Proust. Somewhere.

Section 9: Robert Duncan, *The H. D. Book* (Part 2, Chapter 1). ed. Michael Boughn and Victor Coleman. Berkeley: University of California Press, 2011, 241.

Section 11: "Hey poems we are free to go" is the first line by Michele Leggott from the last poem of her book *Mirabile Dictu*. Auckland, NZ: Auckland University Press 2009, 152.

Mackle, Shard, and Trace

The American Heritage Dictionary definition of mackle: "Printing: A spot, particularly a blurred or double impression caused by a slipping of the type or wrinkle in the paper." My use is a bit more capacious and includes the concept of the "trace."

The owl in the waste places is from Psalm 102.

"Unlikely smattering of themes" is a citation from a student, who was trying to describe poetry.

Angelus Novus

This *locus classicus* of modernity is from Walter Benjamin's 1940 work, "On the Concept of History," trans. Harry Zohn, from *Walter Benjamin, Selected Writings*, Vol. 4: 1938–1940. Cambridge: Harvard University Press, 2003, 392–93. The monoprint on which Benjamin comments is by Paul Klee.

An earlier and more familiar translation by Harry Zohn, giving the title as "Theses on the Philosophy of History," appears in *Illuminations*, ed. with an Introduction by Hannah Arendt. New York: Schocken Books, 1969, 257–58. The gist of the translation is the same; there are slightly different word choices and syntactic emphases. I am using the less familiar translation.

Summer Poem

Title with homage to the title of Hans Magnus Ensenzberger's ruminative poem that I first read in 1970, and which had a serious impact on me.

Citation about birds from Sy Montgomery. *Birdology: Adventures with Hip Hop Parrots, Cantankerous Cassowaries, Crabby Crows, Peripatetic Pigeons, Hens, Hawks, and Hummingbirds*, Free Press 2010.

Otherwise a meditation in part concerning the July 4th week and after in 2016 in the US and elsewhere. There were at least two or three police murders of Black men, and the sniper killing of five Dallas police officers guarding a peaceful Black Lives Matter protest. And there were other slaughters and massacres and killings in the world at large in July 2016.

Late Work

Late Work is part of a multibook long poem called *Traces, with Days*. This is the overarching title for a work in alternating autonomous books. In order, to date the books are *Days and Works*. Boise, Idaho: Ahsahta Press, 2017; this book *Late Work*. NY: Black Square Editions, 2020; *Around the Day in 80 Worlds*. Buffalo, NY: BlazeVOX, 2018. Currently seeking a publisher is *Poetic Realism* [Traces 2].

Acknowledgments

Many thanks to these editors and journals for their interest in this work. Great thanks to John Yau and Black Square Editions and the designer of this book, Shanna Compton. Some of these poems have been revised from their first published versions.

"Shepherd's Calendar." Poems September, October, November, December. *Brooklyn Rail*, Fall 2016, ed. Anselm Berrigan.

"Shepherd's Calendar." Poem May, Spring 2018 from *Lemon Hound*, ed. Sina Queyras.

"Incomplete Enlightenment." *Conjunctions* Online, October 2018. http://www.conjunctions.com/online/article/rachel-blau-duplessis-10-16-2018

"Quality Time," *Cordite* 33: The End, ed. Pam Brown. live Jan 31, 2016, Australia. http://cordite.org.au/content/poetry/theend/?utm_source=-Cordite+Press+Inc+List&utm_cam

"Useful Knots and How to Tie Them." *Conjunctions: 66, Affinity*. Spring/May 2016: 53–61. ed. Bradford Morrow.

"Everyday Life." *Supplement*, ed. Ariel Resnikoff and Orchid Tierney. Published for Programs in Contemporary Writing (University of Pennsylvania) by s.l.: The Materialist Press (2016): 144–150.

"Everyday Life" was also published in French as "La vie au jour le jour," translated by J-P. Auxeméry for K•O•S•H•K•O•N•O•N•G• ed. Jean Daive, Numéro 11, Hiver 2017: 11–19.

"July 31, 2015." In *ATTN: first issue.* ed. Chris Martin, 2015. n.p.

"Per Se." *Journal of Poetics Research* 3, ed. John Tranter, Sept 2015. http://poeticsresearch.com/?article=rachel-blau-duplessis-per-se

"Mackle, Shard, and Trace," *datableed* 6 (Jan.–Feb. 2017). http://www.datableedzine.com/

"Angelus Novus," *Hambone* 22, ed. Nathaniel Mackey. Fall 2019: 270–277. A translation into French (October 2018) by Auxémery. http://www.alligatorzine.be/pages/151/zine194.html

"Summer Poem," *Chicago Review* 60:4 / 61: 1, Fall 2017: 1–11. Some sections in *Resist Much/Obey Little: Inaugural Poems to the Resistance,* coedited Michael Boughn, Kent Johnson, et al.

About the Author

Rachel Blau DuPlessis, poet, critic, collagist, is the author of the multivolume long poem *Drafts*, (1986–2012) and the collage-poems *Graphic Novella* (Xexoxial Editions, 2015) and *NUMBERS* (Materialist Press, 2018). Her newest project is a multibook long poem called *Traces, with Days*. These are *Days and Works* (Ahsahta, 2017), *Late Work* (Black Square Editions, 2020), *Around the Day in 80 Worlds* (BlazeVOX, 2018), and *Poetic Realism* (in circulation). She has written a trilogy of critical essays on gender and poetics: *The Pink Guitar*, *Blue Studios* and *Purple Passages*, and several other critical books. DuPlessis has edited *The Selected Letters of George Oppen*, coedited *The Objectivist Nexus*, and has written extensively on modern and contemporary poetry. Her work has been translated into French and Italian.